Written by Hannah Wilson.
Illustrations by Chris Dickason.
Cover typography based on designs by Thy Bui.

First published in Great Britain in 2023 by Red Shed, part of Farshore

An imprint of HarperCollins*Publishers*
1 London Bridge Street, London SE1 9GF
www.farshore.co.uk

HarperCollins*Publishers*
Macken House, 39/40 Mayor Street Upper,
Dublin 1, D01 C9W8, Ireland

Copyright © HarperCollins*Publishers* Limited 2023

ISBN 978 0 00 861214 6

Printed and bound in the UK using 100% Renewable Electricity at CPI Group (UK) Ltd.
001

A CIP catalogue record for this title is available from the British Library.

Stay safe online. Any website addresses listed in this book are correct at the time of going
to print. However, Farshore is not responsible for content hosted by third parties. Please be
aware that online content can be subject to change and websites can contain content that is
unsuitable for children. We advise that all children are supervised when using the internet.

FSC
www.fsc.org

MIX
Paper | Supporting
responsible forestry
FSC™ C007454

This book is produced from independently certified FSC™ paper
to ensure responsible forest management.

For more information visit: www.harpercollins.co.uk/green

# AMAZING FACTS

## KING CHARLES III

RED SHED

**Did you know?**

Charles is passionate about
the environment.

He was the first royal
to go to school.

Charles once played the cello on TV.

He has a tropical tree frog
named after him.

**Read on to discover over 100 fascinating
and surprising facts about King Charles III,
his family and his royal role!**

## King Charles III is the 13th British monarch.

On 8th September 2022, Charles III became monarch of the United Kingdom (England, Wales, Scotland and Northern Ireland). For many centuries, the different regions within the country were ruled separately. In 1707, Queen Anne became the first monarch to rule over Great Britain (England, Wales and Scotland) as well as Ireland.

## The first king of England ruled over a thousand years ago!

Athelstan, the grandson of Alfred the Great, was the first of a long line of kings to rule over all of England – long before England, Wales, Scotland and Northern Ireland were united as one nation. He came to power in 927.

Queen Mary I

## The first queen of Scotland was Mary Stuart.

Mary Stuart, also known as 'Mary Queen of Scots,' ruled Scotland from 1542 to 1567.

# There have been two other King Charles.

King Charles is called 'the third' (III) because there have been two previous kings called Charles. King Charles I was very unpopular. His rule (and his life) ended when his head was chopped off on 30th January 1649. Ouch!

**King Charles I**                    **King Charles II**

## King Charles was born
## at Buckingham Palace.

In the past, most senior royals were born at home, rather than in hospital. The first direct heir to the British throne to be born in a hospital was the King's son, Prince William.

## Royal births are announced by a notice posted on a golden easel.

Whenever a new baby royal is due, crowds of people gather outside Buckingham Palace, eagerly awaiting notice of the birth. The framed notice, placed on a golden easel, confirms the date and time the baby was born.

## King Charles was once compared to a plum pudding!

When Prince Philip first met his baby son, Charles, he declared that the newborn looked like a plum pudding! Tee hee!

## King Charles has three middle names.

Charles's full name, used on his birth certificate, is Charles Philip Arthur George. The longest name in royal history belonged to Don Alfonso, a great-great-grandson of Charles III of Spain. He had 88 names!

## When King Charles was born, his father was playing squash!

In the past, it was normal for fathers to stay away when their new babies arrived. Prince Philip was playing the ball game squash when Charles was born at Buckingham Palace in 1948.

## King Charles was heir to the throne longer than any royal in British history.

Charles became heir (or next in line) to the throne in 1952 at three years old, when his mother Elizabeth became queen. He finally became king in 2022 after spending 70 years as heir.

## Charles was the oldest British royal to become a monarch.

Charles was 73 years old when he became king after the death of his mother, Elizabeth II, in September 2022. Elizabeth was only 25 years old when she became queen in 1952.

## The youngest monarch in British history was only six days old!

In 1542, Mary Stuart became Queen of Scotland. Mary 'Queen of Scots' was only six days old!

## Kings and queens are crowned at Westminster Abbey.

A 'coronation' is the ceremony at which a new monarch is crowned. Ever since William the Conqueror was crowned in 1066, the monarchs of England and, later, the United Kingdom, have all had their coronations in Westminster Abbey, a vast church near the Houses of Parliament in London.

## The coronation crown is over 300 years old.

That's old! The coronation ceremony involves two different crowns. One of them, the St Edward's crown, was made in 1661 for the coronation of Charles II. It has a solid-gold frame set with semi-precious stones and weighs 2.23kg.

# Elizabeth II's coronation was one of the first major TV events!

It's estimated that over 20 million people watched the coronation of Elizabeth II on black-and-white television. Many households bought TVs for the first time, and people who didn't own a TV went to watch the event with friends or neighbours. It was estimated that every TV in Britain was being watched by an average of seventeen people!

## Thirty kings and queens are buried in Westminster Abbey.

Enclosed in stone tombs or underground vaults, 30 monarchs lie at rest in Westminster Abbey. They include the 'boy king' Edward VI, who was only 15 years old when he died in 1553.

## Westminster Abbey is also used for state funerals.

More than 2,000 people attended the state funeral of Charles's mother, Queen Elizabeth II, at Westminster Abbey.

# The line of mourners queuing to see Queen Elizabeth's coffin reached 16km long.

About a quarter of a million people waited, some for 24 hours, to pay their respects to Queen Elizabeth II, as she lay in state at Westminster Hall, near the Abbey.

## The king's mother, Queen Elizabeth II, was the longest-reigning queen of all time.

Elizabeth held the throne for 70 years and 214 days, from 6th February 1952 until her death on 8th September 2022. Her Platinum Jubilee, marking 70 years on the throne, was celebrated in spring 2022, with parades and street parties in her honour.

**King Charles III**

**Queen Consort Camilla**

# It's impossible to become king or queen by marrying a royal.

It's true! In the UK, if your royal husband or wife is crowned monarch, you would become a consort (companion), but you would not be a king or queen yourself. King Charles's wife, Camilla, is called the Queen Consort. Elizabeth II's husband, Philip, was known as Prince Philip.

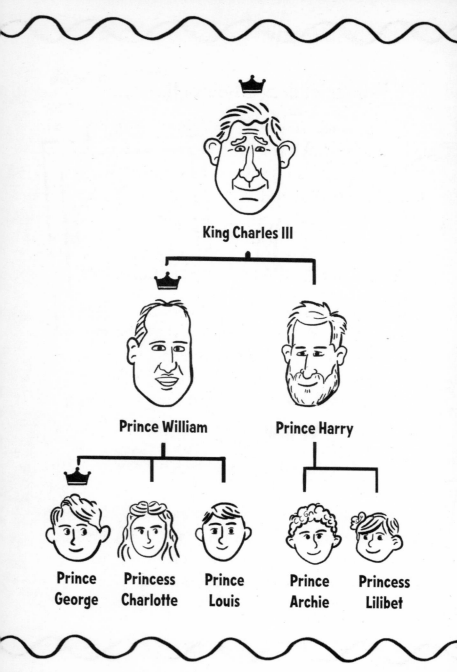

King Charles III

Prince William  Prince Harry

Prince George Princess Charlotte Prince Louis Prince Archie Princess Lilibet

## Prince William is heir to the throne.

Charles has two sons, Prince William and Prince Harry, from his marriage to his first wife, Diana. William, the eldest, will be king after Charles. Next in line is William's eldest child, George.

## King Charles III has five grandchildren.

George, Charlotte and Louis are the children of Prince William and his wife, Catherine. Archie and Lilibet are the children of Prince Harry, and his wife, Meghan.

## King Charles III has five step-grandchildren.

His step-grandchildren are the grandchildren of his second wife, Camilla, now the Queen Consort. Their names are Lola, Frederick, Eliza, Gus and Louis.

## King Charles was the first royal to go to school.

Yes, really! Before Charles started at Hill House school in west London on 7th November 1956, the royal family were all taught at home by tutors.

## Charles was also the first heir to the throne to get a university degree.

In 1970, Charles graduated from Cambridge University, where he had studied archaeology, anthropology (the study of people) and history.

# Charles found out he was going to be the Prince of Wales while watching TV with his school friends.

In July 1958, nine-year-old Charles was watching TV at school. He heard his mother's voice announce that he was going to be made a prince!

## Charles went to school in Australia.

In 1966, the 17-year-old prince spent time
studying at a school outside Melbourne,
Australia. He learnt to chop wood and hike
in the wild bushland.

# The monarch has two birthdays!

In addition to celebrating the day they were born, it's traditional for British kings and queens to have a second 'official' birthday on a different day of the year. A ceremony called Trooping the Colour takes place, where the monarch inspects the royal troops (soldiers) near Buckingham Palace in London.

# The king's birthdays are marked by firing guns.

The tradition of a gun salute to mark important royal occasions began in the 1400s, when ships arriving at ports fired their guns to empty them, showing that they were arriving in peace. Nowadays, historic guns fire 41 rounds to mark the monarch's official birthday. Cover your ears!

## If you reach 100 years old, you might get a birthday message from the king!

It was the Charles's great-grandfather, King George V, who first began the tradition of sending good wishes to all 100 year olds across the land. Today, you have to apply in order to receive a royal greeting!

# The king has visited nearly 100 countries.

Wow! From watching Sumo wrestling tournaments in Japan and kicking footballs in Brazil to celebrating weddings in Spain, King Charles III is a well-travelled royal.

## In just one year, the king can carry out as many as 600 engagements!

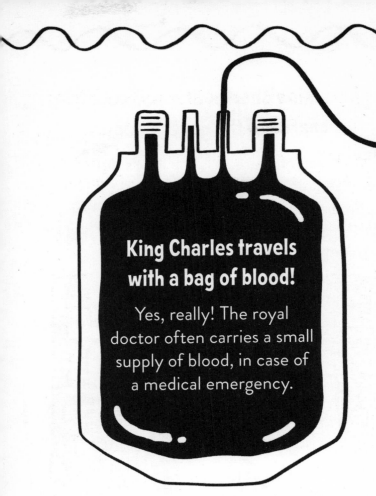

## King Charles travels with a bag of blood!

Yes, really! The royal doctor often carries a small supply of blood, in case of a medical emergency.

## Heirs to the throne don't usually travel together.

This is in case there is an accident.

# King Charles III is not in charge of the government.

As Head of State, it is the king's duty to represent and guide his people – but it is the prime minister, not the king, who leads the UK's government (the politicians who make laws and manage the country).

**Head of State**

**Head of Government**

## The king meets with the prime minister once a week.

For most of the year, the king and the UK's prime minister meet every week at Buckingham Palace. The meeting is completely private. No one knows what they talk about!

# Before the king arrives at the Houses of Parliament, guards search the cellars for explosives!

It's completely true! In 1605, a group including Guy Fawkes tried to blow up London's famous government building by hiding gunpowder in the cellars below. Today, a ceremonial search takes place before the king arrives to formally open a new session of work for the politicians.

Charles is also king in Australia.

As well as being the British monarch, Charles is Head of the Commonwealth, a group of more than 50 countries across the world – several of which, including Australia and Canada, also have him as their monarch.

## Elizabeth II has featured on more coins than any other monarch or leader.

As former Head of the Commonwealth, Queen Elizabeth II's face has appeared on the banknotes and coins of at least 33 different countries!

## The first coin to feature King Charles III was the 50-pence piece.

A few months after Charles became king, the new seven-sided 50-pence piece was minted.
It joined the estimated 29 billion coins already in existence featuring his mother, Queen Elizabeth II.

## The king doesn't vote in elections.

The British monarch must remain neutral, not supporting one political party over another. That's why you'll never see the king posting his paper vote into a ballot box!

## The king is the only person in the UK who can drive a car without a licence!

Now that he is king, Charles can rip up his driver's licence! His official state car doesn't need a licence plate either.

## The king does not need a passport.

When travelling overseas, the king doesn't
need to use a passport – but all other members
of the royal family do.

**Buckingham Palace**

# The King has several official residences.

Home sweet home! The official UK homes of the monarch include Buckingham Palace in London, Windsor Castle in Berkshire, and the Palace of Holyroodhouse in Scotland.

**Palace of Holyroodhouse**

# The king flies a flag to show he's at home.

A flag called the Royal Standard is flown at whichever royal residence the king is staying in.

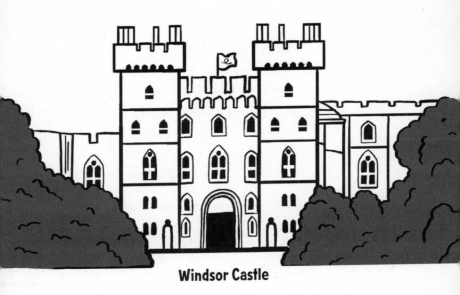

**Windsor Castle**

## Buckingham Palace has 775 rooms.

These include 240 bedrooms and 78 bathrooms!

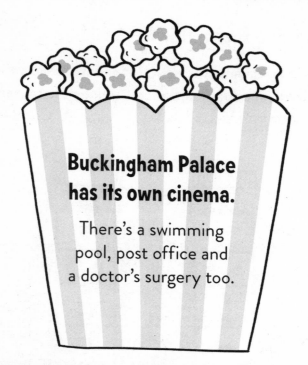

### Buckingham Palace has its own cinema.

There's a swimming pool, post office and a doctor's surgery too.

## Buckingham Palace has over 600 clocks.

When the clocks go back or forward, a special team of royal clock-changers gets to work!

## Newlywed royals greet the crowds from a balcony.

After a royal wedding, it's tradition for the newlyweds to greet the crowds from the balcony of Buckingham Palace. A crowd of over 600,000 people stood on the streets of central London to celebrate the wedding of Charles to his first wife, Diana, in 1981.

## Charles and Diana's wedding was watched across the globe.

An extraordinary 750 million people in 74 countries tuned in to watch Charles and Diana's lavish wedding on TV.

## Buckingham Palace used to be called . . . Buckingham House.

Buckingham Palace has been the main London home for the royal family since 1837, when Queen Victoria came to the throne. It started out as a much smaller house, built in the early 1700s by the Duke of Buckingham – before being transformed into today's magnificent royal residence.

## Windsor Castle is the largest lived-in castle in the world.

Kings and queens have been living in this vast castle for almost 1,000 years. The banqueting hall alone is longer than two tennis courts – with a table that can seat up to 162 guests!

## The number of people working in one castle kitchen is the same as three football teams!

Up to 33 members of staff, including chefs and washer-uppers, work hard in the Great Kitchen at Windsor Castle. The clocks there are set five minutes ahead of real time to make sure dinner is never late!

## In 1992, a fire destroyed 115 rooms at Windsor Castle.

After a faulty spotlight set fire to a curtain, flames raced through the ancient building. It took 225 firefighters about 15 hours – and 6.8 million litres of water – to put it out. Phew!

## Charles must never be called 'Your Royal Highness'.

When Charles was Prince of Wales, people could greet him as 'Sir' or 'Your Royal Highness'. Now he is king, they must remember to call him 'Your Majesty'.

## The royals are not supposed to sign autographs.

This is to stop people from copying and faking their signatures.

# It's traditional to bow or curtsy to the king.

It's not usual for people to touch a member of the royal family. However, Melanie Brown, or 'Mel B', from the famous pop group the Spice Girls, planted a kiss on the surprised prince's cheek when he met the group in 1997!

## Before 1917, the royals didn't have a surname.

Really? It's true! In 1917, King George V, Charles's great-grandfather, chose the surname Windsor, named after the royal castle. Today, some royals use the surname Mountbatten-Windsor. Mountbatten was the surname of King Charles's father, Prince Philip.

## Prince Harry is actually Prince Henry!

Charles's youngest son's real name is Henry Charles Albert David . . . but everyone calls him Harry!

## Meghan's real name is Rachel.

Meghan, Duchess of Sussex, was born
Rachel Meghan Markle.

## Catherine, Princess of Wales,
## had the nickname Squeak!

Pip and Squeak were the names of the two pet
guinea pigs at Catherine's school. As Catherine's
younger sister is called Pippa (Pip),
Catherine's friends nicknamed *her* Squeak!

## Prince Harry named his daughter after his grandmother.

When Prince Harry and Meghan had their second child in June 2021, they called her Lilibet, the nickname of Elizabeth II. As a toddler, when Elizabeth tried to say her own name, it sounded like 'Lilibet'!

Hello, Bertie . . .

I mean, Arthur . . .

I mean, GEORGE!

## Monarchs sometimes change their name.

Seems strange? It's actually quite common
for a new king or queen to choose a different
name when they are crowned. The full name
of Charles's grandfather was Albert Frederick
Arthur George. His family and friends called him
'Bertie', but he chose to be called King George.

## The king's special symbol uses the letters C and R.

The special symbol is called a 'cypher' and it combines the letters C and R and the numeral III. The C is for Charles, and the R is for Rex, the Latin word for 'king'. III represents three – he's the third King of England to be called Charles. The cypher is used on buildings, documents and even postboxes.

## The king wakes up to the sound of bagpipes!

Every morning, a piper plays for 15 minutes outside the king's window. Queen Victoria first introduced the tradition in 1843, and since then there have been 17 different 'Pipe Majors' performing this important musical duty!

## The king has his very own tartan.

Tartan is a type of cloth design. The special Balmoral tartan is grey, black and red, and apart from the king, only the Pipe Major and pipers on the Balmoral Estate, in Scotland, are allowed to wear it. Sometimes, other royals may wear the tartan – but they have to ask permission from the king first!

# King Charles III is famous for his charity work.

Charles has founded or supported more than 420 different charities. Their work includes protecting Asian elephants, helping surfers stop sewage being pumped into oceans, and supporting doctors who fly to remote parts of Australia.

Helo, fy enw
i yw Charles.

## King Charles can speak Welsh.

Well, a little bit! Before he became king,
Charles used to be the Prince of Wales. Ever
since his first public speech in Welsh in 1969,
King Charles has tried to add a little of the
language into speeches that take place in Wales.
Da iawn, y Brenin Charles!

## King Charles cares about the environment.

King Charles has worked towards protecting our planet for more than 50 years, warning about air pollution caused by cars and the problem with plastic waste. In 2007, he was presented with an award by Harvard University, in the USA, honouring him as 'a leading international voice in protecting the natural world'.

## The king has many feathered friends.

Pecking around the gardens at the king's home Highgrove House are Charles's prized Burford Brown and Maran chickens. If he has time, Charles feeds them and collects their eggs.

## Charles likes to shake hands with trees!

Or perhaps should that be 'shake branches'?
After tree-planting ceremonies, the king gives a
branch a gentle shake to wish it well.

# The king loves . . . hedges!

Hedges are important habitats for wildlife, and 'hedge laying' is a way of creating and maintaining them. King Charles is a skilled hedge layer. He even hosted a hedge-laying championship at his farm near Tetbury in the Cotswolds!

## The king has a car that runs on wine and cheese!

Sounds strange? It's true! The king's car runs on a fuel called E85, made from leftover wine, and whey from the cheese-making process! Whey-hey!

# King Charles built a town.

Yes, really! Working with a team of architects and planners, King Charles helped to create the town of Poundbury, near Dorchester. It is built on land that he owned as Prince of Wales.

Work began in 1993 and Poundbury is now home to 4,000 people – some of whom call it 'Charlestown' after its founder.

## Charles has musical talent!

As a schoolboy, Charles played the piano, trumpet and cello.

## Charles once played the cello on TV.

When a film about royal family life was shown on TV in 1969, it showed Charles practising his cello. One of the strings of the instrument broke in the face of Charles's brother Edward. Ouch!

## Henry VIII also loved music.

Charles isn't the only musical royal.
Tudor king Henry VIII famously played many
instruments, including the lute, organ, recorder,
flute and harp. He had a vast collection
of musical instruments, including over
150 recorders!

# The king often has a sword by his side.

For formal occasions, the king may wear a red coat, decorated with a blue sash and numerous medals from his military career. A ceremonial sword hangs by his side.

## Charles can fly a plane.

Like many members of the Royal Family,
Charles has served in the military. While in the
Royal Air Force (RAF), Charles was trained
to fly helicopters and to pilot a jet. He also
served in the Royal Navy.

## Prince William has flown 156 rescue missions as a helicopter pilot.

Charles's sons, William and Harry, also had military careers. William worked for three years with the RAF Search and Rescue team. Once, he responded to an emergency call in just 38 seconds, rescuing two girls who had been washed out to sea.

## Prince Harry set up a sports competition for injured servicemen and women.

Prince Harry spent 10 years in the British Army. In 2013, he founded the Invictus Games, a bit like an Olympic Games, for the brave men and women who were injured or became ill while working in the Armed Forces. During the first games in London in 2014, more than 400 people competed for medals in athletics, swimming, sailing and team sports.

# The former Prince of Wales is now the King of Whales!

Because of a law dating back to 1324, the king owns all the whales and dolphins found in waters up to about 5km from the British shoreline!

## The king also owns swans.

Weird but true! Since the 1100s, the monarch has had the right to claim all the unmarked mute swans swimming in British open waters. Long ago, royals and other wealthy folk would eat swans, but today the wild birds are protected by the king and his royal Swan Keeper.

## The king is a Keeper of the Cows.

In 2011, Charles was given the title 'Keeper of the Cows' by the Maasai people in Tanzania in honour of his long history supporting farming.

## There's a tropical tree frog named after Charles!

Hopping around the steamy cloud forests of Ecuador in central America is a little, orange-spotted frog called *Hyloscirtus princecharlesi*. It was named after Charles to honour his work protecting rainforests.

## Queen Elizabeth II was once given an elephant as a present!

In 1972, when Elizabeth II was visiting Cameroon, in central Africa, the president gave her an elephant. Jumbo the elephant ate bananas, avocados and sugar on the flight back to England, where he soon found a home at London Zoo.

## Charles was charged at by an elephant!

Eek! The king said it was scary when he was charged at by a bull (male) elephant while in Kenya. Luckily, Charles escaped unharmed.

## The king once got into a flap with a bald eagle!

At a flower show in 2015, Charles met Zephyr, a bald eagle being held by a handler. Suddenly, Zephyr stretched out and flapped his enormous 120cm-wide wings, startling the bemused royal!

## King Charles couldn't quite stomach a live witchetty grub!

In Australia, in 2005, Charles was offered a tasty traditional snack – a live witchetty grub (the caterpillar of a moth). He politely declined to eat the bug.

## The king and queen consort love dogs.

Charles's wife, Camilla, adopted two rescue dogs,
Bluebell and Beth, both Jack Russell terriers,
in 2017. She also works with a charity that
trains dogs to sniff out cancer!

Many years earlier, Charles and his family owned
two Jack Russell terriers called Pooh and Tigga.
Sadly, Pooh got lost in the countryside near
Balmoral Castle, but Tigga lived happily
alongside Charles for 18 years.

# Cavalier King Charles spaniels have nothing to do with King Charles.

Well, not King Charles III, anyway!
It's thought that these furry, long-eared dogs
were named after King Charles II in the 1600s.

**King Charles II**

**King Charles spaniel**

## The royal family loves horses.

The royals have a long history of owning and riding horses. Charles's first racehorse was called Allibar. Charles bought Allibar in 1980 and entered his first race as a jockey soon after.

## Charles trained to be a jockey by riding a bicycle with no seat!

When horse racing, the jockeys don't sit down, so a saddle-less bike was great for training!

## The queen's favourite pony attended her funeral.

Elizabeth II also loved horses and is thought to have owned as many as 100 horses and ponies in her lifetime. Emma, a glossy black pony, stood with her groom on the route of the funeral procession that took Elizabeth's coffin to Windsor Castle. One of the queen's headscarves was draped over her saddle.

# King Charles believes in horsepower!

When trees fall down in the woodlands around Balmoral Castle in Scotland, Charles likes to remove them in a traditional, environmentally friendly way – using horses. When horses move the trees, they cause less damage to the forest than a machine would. Tree-mendous!

# King Charles once broke his arm by falling off a horse.

In 1990, Charles tumbled from his horse during a polo match, a game a bit like hockey played on horseback. With a broken right arm, the poorly prince needed help from his assistant. It's said that his toothpaste had to be squeezed for him!

# Charles met Camilla at a polo match.

The king met his second wife, Camilla, at a polo match in 1970. After marriages to other people, they got married to each other in 2005.

## Prince William has a polo-playing disadvantage.

For Prince William, hitting the ball with a stick while balancing on a horse is harder than it is for many other players. Polo rules state that the stick must be swung with your right hand, but the Prince is . . . left-handed!

## Catherine, the Princess of Wales, has an even bigger polo disadvantage.

She's allergic to horses! Achoo!

# King Charles once scuba-dived to see a shipwreck.

In 1545, King Henry VIII watched his famous warship, the *Mary Rose*, sink off the coast of Portsmouth during a sea battle with France. The wreck laid untouched on the seabed for over 400 years until it was discovered by archaeologists in 1971. A few years later, in 1975, Charles joined a team of scuba-divers who swam down to explore the wreck!

## Charles isn't the only royal to enjoy scuba-diving . . .

Catherine, Princess of Wales, has qualified as an advanced scuba diver. In 2015, she swam with sharks in the Caribbean Sea to raise awareness about protecting ocean wildlife.

### Charles is a talented artist.

When the king goes on his travels, he often packs
a paintbrush to bring inspiring landscapes to life.
His watercolour paintings of mountains
in Morocco, forests in Canada and castles in
Turkey have been displayed in exhibitions to
raise money for charity.

# King Charles is a published author.

As well as writing books about the natural world, Charles has written an illustrated children's book, inspired by the stories he used to tell his younger brothers when they were children.

# King Charles used to make biscuits.

The Duchy Originals company was founded by Charles in 1990 to champion organic farming. The first product the company ever made was – you've guessed it – biscuits. Oat biscuits, to be precise. The Waitrose Duchy Organic brand is still found on shelves today and includes fruit, vegetables, meat, cheese, and even ice cream.

## King Charles is well known for getting the giggles!

It's not always a serious business being king. When a large bumblebee flew inside Charles's jacket while he was visiting a wildlife sanctuary, he and Camilla couldn't stop laughing!

# King Charles is a magician!

Well, sort of . . . In 1975, after performing a cup-and-balls trick, Charles was invited to join the Magic Circle, a mysterious society of magicians whose members have included some of the most famous magicians of all time.

## Charles was almost swept away by an avalanche.

When skiing with friends in Switzerland in 1988, a huge avalanche of snow came tumbling down the mountainside. Charles managed to get out of the way just in time. Phew!

## The king can ice-skate!

Charles learnt to skate at a rink in west London, and at age 13, was awarded a certificate to prove it!

## Charles and Camilla have starred in a comic!

In 2013, the two royals appeared on the pages of one of the UK's most famous children's comics, the *Beano*!

## The king once presented the weather forecast on TV.

In May 2012, Charles presented the weather for BBC Scotland. Unfortunately, there was no good news – it was a cold, wet, windy day!

## Charles is King of the Cobbles!

In 2000, Charles appeared on the TV soap opera
*Coronation Street*. He didn't actually walk down
the famous cobbled street – he appeared in
a fictional TV news report. He was on the telly –
on the telly!

**Look out for other books in the series!**

KING CHARLES III

**All the facts! All the fun!**